See Me

See Me

BEYOND THE CLASSROOM

Kim Biddle

Illustrated by Jeremy Goolman

gatekeeper press™
Columbus, Ohio

Enjoy -

Kim Biddle

9-16-21

See Me: Beyond the Classroom

Published by Gatekeeper Press
2167 Stringtown Rd, Suite 109
Columbus, OH 43123-2989
www.GatekeeperPress.com

Library of Congress Control Number: 2020943619

ISBN (hardcover): 9781662903625
ISBN (paperback): 9781662903632
eISBN: 9781662903649

In memory of my great niece Evie Claire Rigdon.

Matthew 18:5 And whoever welcomes one such child in my name welcomes me.

I saw you today.

I sat quietly on your bus.
Although others were talking,
you didn't scream or fuss.

I saw you today.

You're the one who
makes the rules.
Did you even notice me
walking through the school?

I saw you today.

I handed you my note.
I've been absent for days
because I didn't have a coat.

I saw you today.

You said, "Let's take a walk."
Once I saw your badge,
I knew I shouldn't talk.

I saw you today.

You were wiping down your door.
I wonder if you have a
Soft, warm bed,
while I sleep on the
cold, hard floor.

I saw you today.

Oh, I wish I could stay.
A nice warm meal to fill my tummy,
the last I'll have today.

I saw you today.

You gave me some
shoes and clothes.
I had trouble walking
from the small shoes
that hurt my toes.

I saw you today.

I told you that I fell.
You saw my marks and bruises.
I hoped you wouldn't tell!

I saw you today.

You seemed concerned and kind.
I do fear when we talk,
what you may really find.

I saw you today.

I was sitting at my desk.
I wasn't thinking about
your lessons,
homework assignments,
or state test.

I saw you all today.

Is education really free?

What is the point?

If you truly don't SEE ME!

CPSIA information can be obtained
at www.ICGtesting.com
Printed in the USA
LVRC102243020621
689201LV00003B/22